FARMALL SUPER SERIES
PHOTO ARCHIVE

FARMALL SUPER SERIES

PHOTO ARCHIVE
Super A, Super C, Super H, and Super M

Photographs from the
McCormick-International Harvester Company Collection

Edited with introduction by
P.A. Letourneau

Iconografix
Photo Archive Series

Iconografix
PO Box 609
Osceola, Wisconsin 54020 USA

Library of Congress Card Number 96-76057

ISBN 1-882256-49-2

96 97 98 99 00 5 4 3 2 1

Cover design by Lou Gordon, Osceola, Wisconsin
Digital imaging by Pixelperfect, Madison, Wisconsin

Printed in the United States of America

Book trade distribution by Voyageur Press, Inc. (800) 888-9653

PREFACE

The histories of machines and mechanical gadgets are contained in the books, journals, correspondence and personal papers stored in libraries and archives throughout the world. Written in tens of languages, covering thousands of subjects, the stories are recorded in millions of words.

Words are powerful. Yet, the impact of a single image, a photograph or an illustration, often relates more than dozens of pages of text. Fortunately, many of the libraries and archives that house the words also preserve the images.

In the *Photo Archive Series,* Iconografix reproduces photographs and illustrations selected from public and private collections. The images are chosen to tell a story—to capture the character of their subject. Reproduced as found, they are accompanied by the captions made available by the archive.

The *Iconografix Photo Archive Series* is dedicated to young and old alike, the enthusiast, the collector and anyone who, like us, is fascinated by " things" mechanical.

The photographs and illustrations that appear in this book were made available by The State Historical Society of Wisconsin. The Society is the official repository for records of the International Harvester Company and its nineteenth-century predecessor, the McCormick Harvesting Machine Company.

The McCormick-International Harvester Company Collection contains nearly 4,000 cubic feet of family papers and business records, including technical publications, advertising literature, engineering and promotional photographs, posters, and films. Its cataloguing, preservation, and administration are funded through an endowment established in 1991 by Brooks McCormick.

Use of the collection is not generally restricted. However, due to its size and complexity, interested persons are encouraged to contact the Society in advance, at 816 State Street, Madison, Wisconsin 53706.

Waycross, Georgia farmer and International Harvester dealer discuss the merits of the Farmall Super A.

INTRODUCTION

US farm tractor production was severely curtailed during World War II. The industrial capacities of the major manufacturers were largely directed toward production of military tractors or other machinery and munitions. Raw materials, such as rubber, copper, steel, and bronze—the basic components of heavy manufacturing—were simply not available for civilian goods, even if such goods were critical to food production.

After the war, the pent-up demand for new tractors was enormous. Farm income had risen, and farmers were eager to replace their worn machinery. Generally, post-war tractors were the same models offered prior to the war. Little money or time had been invested in new model development. With few notable exceptions, the tractors of the post-war period were designed in the early to mid-1930s. They would remain in production until the early to mid-1950s.

The Models A, B, H, and M were introduced in 1939, the last new series of Farmall tractors prior to the war. The first new post-war models, the Farmall Cub and Farmall C, were introduced in 1947 and 1948, respectively. Although popular, neither was particularly innovative in design. The Cub was a scaled-down version of the Model A; the C, an updated version of the B, built with an operator's platform. (International's hydraulic Touch-Control, optional on the Model C, would be a standard feature of the subsequent Super C.)

The company's work on a new series of Farmalls resumed with earnest by 1946. The new tractors would not be ready before 1954, however. To meet growing demands for greater horsepower and improvements in hydraulics, electrics, and safety features, IH introduced modernized versions of the existing line. The Super A was the first of the "new" Farmalls. Introduced in 1947, it featured the same 4-speed transmission and choice of gasoline or distillate engine as did the A. However, the engine operated at a higher speed which boosted output. The

Super A was also fitted with hydraulic Touch-Control. It was built in four distinct versions: the International Super A, which has every appearance of being a taller and heavier machine, better suited to industrial applications; the Farmall Super A, the most common configuration; the Super A1, a late-production Super A that offered improved hydraulics; and the Super AV, a high clearance model commonly used in tall vegetables. The Super A remained in production through 1954.

The Super C appeared in 1951 and was built through 1954. It featured an engine of greater displacement than that of the C that produced a significant boost in horsepower. The Super C offered a new disk brake system, a shock-absorbing seat, and standard Touch-Control hydraulics. The Super C was available with either tricycle front or adjustable wide-front.

The Super H and high-clearance Super HV were the last of the Farmall Super Series to be introduced. Built only in 1953 and 1954, they were distinguished from their predecessors by an increase in engine displacement that boosted horsepower by more than 25 percent. New disk brakes were also added. The Super H was offered with either tricycle front or adjustable wide-front.

The Super M, diesel Super MD, and the high-clearance Super MV and Super MDV were built from 1952 through 1954. The Super M-TA, its diesel companion Super M-TAD, and the high-clearance Super M-TAV and diesel Super M-TADV, were built only in 1954. The Super M, offered as a gasoline or LPG tractor, featured a larger displacement engine than its predecessor and a corresponding 20 percent greater horsepower. The Super MD also benefited from greater displacement and offered 30 percent greater output. The Super M-TA and it's derivatives were simply Super M, MV, MD, and MDVs fitted with a torque amplifier that allowed a half-step power downshift. In effect, it created ten speeds forward, rather than the five speeds of the standard Super Ms.

Farmall Super Series Photo Archive includes a variety of photographs that illustrate this popular series of tractors at work in the most common applications.

Farmall and International Super A
1947 - 1954

Two views of a Super A planting corn with Model A-178 planter. Waycross, Georgia, March 1952.

Attaching planter seed plate drive to a Super A.

Filling POAX reverse feed hopper with cotton seed, on a Super A with Model A-177 Blackland planter.

Super A with Model A-435 4-row rear-mounted vegetable planter.

Super A with Model A-674 forward-mounted vegetable planter.

Super A with Model A-178 cotton and corn planter with single hopper and fertilizer attachment.

Super A with Model A-178 cotton and corn planter with duplex hopper and fertilizer attachment.

Two views of a Super A cultivating an unidentified crop.

Super A and Farmall Cub hauling lumber at a Clayton, Georgia mill. December 1950.

Super A hauling lumber inside a Clayton, Georgia mill. December 1950.

Two views of a Super A with Model A1-23 mower owned by the Evanston, Illinois Park Department. July 1951.

Super A with leveling and grader blade in snow.

Super A with leveling and grader blade cleaning a feedlot.

Super A, with leveling and grader blade mounted behind front wheels, cleaning a shallow ditch.

International Super A cutting grass along a farm-to-market road near Fort Deposit, Alabama.

Two views of the first International Super A, with Model A1-23 highway mower, near Baton Rouge, Louisiana.

30

Super A industrial with Hough power broom at Fort Lauderdale, Florida.

Two Super A's with Lilliston mowers. Savanah, Georgia airport, February 1952.

Super A used to haul lumber from a rail siding to a Dubach, Louisiana lumber yard.

International Super A1, owned by the Illinois Central Railroad, mowing the right-of-way near Alma, Illinois.

Farmall Super C
1951 - 1954

Illustrations of two views of the Super C.

Super C with Model C-254 2-row cultivator.

Super C with Model C-254 2-row cultivator and #10 tooling equipment. German Valley, Illinois.

Super C supplying power for post hole auger.

Super C and 2-bottom plow.

Two views of a wide front Super C and 2-bottom plow.

Super C with leveling and grader blade doing soil conservation work on a farm near Saginaw, Michigan.

Super C with leveling and grader blade grading a farm road near Saginaw, Michigan. September 1951.

Planting and fertilizing with a Super C and Model C-278 planter.

Super C with Touch-Control and C-278 runner-type planter with single-seed hopper and fertilizer attachments.

Super C with C-254 cultivator and #91 spring-tooth rear attachment cultivating tobacco.

Super C and C-254 cultivator with #13 tooling equipment and #91 spring-tooth harrow in shade-grown tobacco.

Two veiws of a Super C with 2-bottom plow.

Super C with C-254 cultivator and #310 fertilizer unit in contoured corn. Pella, Iowa, June 1951.

Planting and fertilizing cotton with a Super C and C-278 runner-type planter.

Super C and C-254 2-row cultivator in checked corn. Edgerton, Wisconsin.

Planting and fertilizing with a C-278 planter.

Worm's eye view of a Super C and C-254 2-row cultivator with fertilizer unit cultivating and side-dressing cotton.

Wide front Super C cultivating an unidentified crop.

Super C and C-254 2-row cultivator with #6 rotary weeder in soybeans at Hinsdale Farm.

Super C with C-254 cultivator in checked corn.

Breaktime for a dad and his Super C.

Worm's eye view of a Super C with C-254 cultivator in corn.

Driver's eye view from the seat of the Super C.

Model C-254A corn and cotton cultivator on a Super C.

Super C with 2-point hitch and and C-254 cultivator with sweeps.

Rear and side views of a Super C with 2-point hitch and C-254 cultivator with sweeps.

Driving Super C in position before mounting front cultivator gangs of a Model C-254 cultivator.

Loosening Touch-Control link rod from frame before swinging back to attach Touch-Control power arm.

Attaching C-254 cultivator rear section. Note the built-in kick stands.

Super C with C-254 2-row cultivator in corn.

Super C and C-254 cultivator with 7-1/2-foot weeder-mulcher in corn.

Super C and C-254 cultivator with #10 rotary weeders and 4-section weeder-mulcher. June 1951.

Spreading manure with a Super C equipped with front-mounted leveling and grader blade.

Super C and C-254 cultivator with 7-1/2-foot weeder-mulcher in corn.

Digging a shallow drainage ditch with a Super C and pre-production leveling and grader blade. November 1951.

Super C with Model 64 combine.

Super C with Model 24-P mounted corn picker

Super C with Model C-110 1-row corn picker.

Super C, Model 64 combine, and an International pickup.

Super C with Model 64 combine.

Super C and a Model 64 combine.

Super C, Model 64 combine, and a 1953 International pickup.

Super C and Model 1-PR corn picker.

Super H and Super HV
1953 - 1954

Super H with cultivator.

Super H with cultivator and fertilizer attachment.

Two views of a Super H and Model 64 combine.

Two views of a Super H and Model 64 combine.

Illustration of a high-clearance Super HV.

Super M, Super MD, and Super MTA
1952 - 1954

Illustration of a Super MD.

Illustration of a Super M.

Super M with unidentified plow.

Super M with front-mounted cultivator.

Super M with front-mounted cultivator.

High-clearance Super MTA with Model 34HM-656-2 vegetable cultivator equipped with asparagus bedder disks.

Super M with front-mounted cultivator.

Bird's eye view of a Super M with rotary cultivator.

Super M cultivating checked-row corn.

Super M with disk harrow.

Super MD with unidentified cultivator.

Two views of a Super M cultivating corn.

Two views of a Super M cultivating beans.

Two views of a Super MD cultivating beans.

Super MTA with Model M33 power loader.

Super M with Model HMC-20 cotton stripper.

Two Super M's with Model 64 combines.

Two views of a Super M with Model 64 combine.

Super MTA with Model 192-M corn picker.

Super MTA with Model 140 combine.

Super MTA with Model 4-M beet harvester.

Super MD with Model 140 combine.

Super MTA with unidentified cultivator.

The Iconografix Photo Archive Series includes:

TRACTORS AND CONSTRUCTION EQUIPMENT

CASE TRACTORS 1912-1959 Photo Archive	ISBN 1-882256-32-8	OLIVER TRACTORS Photo Archive	ISBN 1-882256-09-3
CATERPILLAR MILITARY TRACTORS		RUSSELL GRADERS Photo Archive	ISBN 1-882256-11-5
VOLUME 1 Photo Archive	ISBN 1-882256-16-6	TWIN CITY TRACTOR Photo Archive	ISBN 1-882256-06-9
CATERPILLAR MILITARY TRACTORS		**TRUCKS**	
VOLUME 2 Photo Archive	ISBN 1-882256-17-4	DODGE TRUCKS 1929-1947 Photo Archive	ISBN 1-882256-36-0
CATERPILLAR SIXTY Photo Archive	ISBN 1-882256-05-0	DODGE TRUCKS 1948-1960 Photo Archive	ISBN 1-882256-37-9
CATERPILLAR THIRTY Photo Archive	ISBN 1-882256-04-2	MACK MODEL AB Photo Archive	ISBN 1-882256-18-2
CLETRAC AND OLIVER CRAWLERS		MACK MODEL B 1953-1966 VOLUME 1	
Photo Archive	ISBN 1-882256-43-3	Photo Archive	ISBN 1-882256-19-0
FARMALL F-SERIES Photo Archive	ISBN 1-882256-02-6	MACK MODEL B 1953-1966 VOLUME 2	
FARMALL MODEL H Photo Archive	ISBN 1-882256-03-4	Photo Archive	ISBN 1-882256-34-4
FARMALL MODEL M Photo Archive	ISBN 1-882256-15-8	MACK EB-EC-ED-EE-EF-EG & DE 1936-1951	
FARMALL REGULAR Photo Archive	ISBN 1-882256-14-X	Photo Archive	ISBN 1-882256-29-8
FARMALL SUPER SERIES Photo Archive	ISBN 1-882256-49-2	MACK EH-EJ-EM-EQ-ER-ES 1936-1950	
FORDSON 1917-1928 Photo Archive	ISBN 1-882256-33-6	Photo Archive	ISBN 1-882256-39-5
HART-PARR Photo Archive	ISBN 1-882256-08-5	MACK FC, FCSW & NW1936-1947	
HOLT TRACTORS Photo Archive	ISBN 1-882256-10-7	Photo Archive	ISBN 1-882256-28-X
INTERNATIONAL TRACTRACTORS		MACK FG-FH-FJ-FK-FN-FP-FT-FW 1937-1950	
Photo Archive	ISBN 1-882256-48-4	Photo Archive	ISBN 1-882256-35-2
JOHN DEERE MODEL A Photo Archive	ISBN 1-882256-12-3	MACK LF-LH-LJ-LM-LT 1940-1956	
JOHN DEERE MODEL B Photo Archive	ISBN 1-882256-01-8	Photo Archive	ISBN 1-882256-38-7
JOHN DEERE MODEL D Photo Archive	ISBN 1-882256-00-X	STUDEBAKER TRUCKS 1927-1940	
JOHN DEERE 30 SERIES Photo Archive	ISBN 1-882256-13-1	Photo Archive	ISBN 1-882256-40-9
MINNEAPOLIS-MOLINE U-SERIES		STUDEBAKER TRUCKS 1941-1964	
Photo Archive	ISBN 1-882256-07-7	Photo Archive	ISBN 1-882256-41-7

The Iconografix Photo Archive Series is available from direct mail specialty book dealers and bookstores worldwide, or can be ordered from the publisher. For additional information or to add your name to our mailing list contact:

Iconografix
PO Box 609
Osceola, Wisconsin 54020 USA

Telephone: (715) 294-2792
(800) 289-3504 (USA)
Fax: (715) 294-3414

Book trade distribution by Voyageur Press, Inc., PO Box 338, Stillwater, Minnesota 55082 USA   (800) 888-9653

INTERNATIONAL Trac Tractors
PHOTO ARCHIVE
Edited by P. A. Letourneau

MORE GREAT BOOKS FROM ICONOGRAFIX

INTERNATIONAL TRACTRACTORS
Photo Archive
ISBN 1-882256-48-4

FARMALL REGULAR Photo Archive
ISBN 1-882256-14-X

FARMALL F-SERIES Photo Archive
ISBN 1-882256-02-6

FARMALL MODEL H Photo Archive
ISBN 1-882256-03-4

CASE TRACTORS 1912-1959
Photo Archive
ISBN 1-882256-32-8

FARMALL MODEL M Photo Archive
ISBN 1-882256-15-8

FORDSON 1917-1928 Photo Archive
ISBN 1-882256-33-6

FARMALL REGULAR
PHOTO ARCHIVE

Edited by P. A. Letourneau

FARMALL F-SERIES
PHOTO ARCHIVE
Edited by P. A. Letourneau

FARMALL MODEL H
PHOTO ARCHIVE
Edited by P. A. Letourneau

CASE TRACTORS
1912-1959 PHOTO ARCHIVE
Edited by P. A. Letourneau

FARMALL MODEL M
PHOTO ARCHIVE
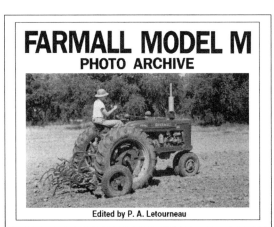
Edited by P. A. Letourneau

FORDSON
1917-1928 PHOTO ARCHIVE
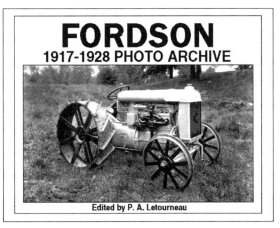
Edited by P. A. Letourneau